Travel BINGO Highway

Dear Travel Adventurers,

Congratulations on purchasing your very own Travel Bingo book! You have chosen an adventure that will provide you with lots of fun and entertainment during your travels.

Be ready to discover the world in a playful way and experience unforgettable moments!With the Travel Bingo book in your hands, you will become true explorers. W

hether you're traveling with family, friends or alone, this book promises hours of laughs, competition and shared memories.Let us enrich your travels in a whole new way. Imagine sitting in your car, anxiously searching for the exciting things pictured on your bingo sheet. Every glance out the window becomes an exciting opportunity to set the next bingo cross. The windmill in the field, the mobile home, the church in the distance or the hamburger on the advertising sign - all these and much more are waiting to be discovered by you.

So, dear travel adventurers, grab your travel bingo book, find a starting point and let's hit the road together. Your travel experiences will never be the same. Let's laugh, compete, and hit the streets!

We wish you an unforgettable time full of fun and exciting discoveries with your travel bingo book.

Get ready to conquer the world and enjoy your travels in a new way. Your adventure starts now!

Game instructions for single players:

Find your bingo sheet from the book and grab a pen. You're ready to rock the road!

Pick a starting point or let your fellow riders give you the "GO" and hit the gas! The journey begins!

Keep your eyes open and look for things on your bingo sheet.

When you spot something, call it out loud and say which way it is. For example, "Windmill in the field to our left!"

Cross off the item you spotted - only then do you get to find a new item in your area! Can you make a horizontal or vertical row on your bingo sheet? Bingo! You are the champion of the street!

Special Challenge: Who will make the best time in Travel Bingo? Time yourself and record your best time.

Who will beat you next time and become champion of the road?

Game instructions for several players:

Each player gets his own bingo sheet and a pen. A small pair of scissors helps ... Departure!

Choose a starting point and go full throttle! The hunt for the bingo items begins!

When a player spots an item on their sheet, they shout it out and give directions. Example: "The tow truck in the oncoming lane." Let the others know where it's going!

Grab the spotted item and make a check mark. No one else is allowed to dust it off! Once you're done then it's on to the next.

Does a player have a row from left to right or top to bottom? Bingo!

End of the round. Who was the fastest player? The king or queen of the road is crowned!

Now it's getting wild on the street! Fun, competition, and lots of laughs await you with the Car Bingo book. Whether you're driving alone or with your road trip buddies, this trip will be legendary! So grab the book, turn on the engine, and experience unforgettable adventures on the road! Caution: Addictive!

Name .... Time ....

Travel BINGO Highway

Name .... **Time** ....

Travel BINGO Highway

Name		Time		

Travel BINGO

Highway

Travel BINGO Highway

Name .... Time ....

Travel BINGO

Highway

Name .... Time ....

Travel BINGO
Highway

Travel BINGO
Highway

Name .... Time ....

Travel BINGO
Highway

Travel BINGO Highway

Name .... Time ....

Travel BINGO Highway

Travel BINGO Highway

Travel BINGO

Highway

Travel BINGO
Highway

Name .... Time ....

Travel BINGO Highway

Name .... **Time** ....

Travel BINGO Highway

Name .... **Time** ....

Travel BINGO Highway

Travel BINGO Highway

Travel BINGO
Highway

Name .... Time ....

Travel BINGO Highway

Name		Time		

Name .... **Time** ....

Travel BINGO
Highway

Name .... Time ....

Travel BINGO Highway

Name .... Time ....

Travel BINGO Highway

Travel BINGO
Highway

Name .... Time ....

Travel BINGO
Highway

Name .... **Time** ....

Travel BINGO Highway

Name	Time

Travel BINGO Highway

Travel BINGO
Highway

Travel BINGO Highway

Name .... Time ....

Travel BINGO
Highway

Name .... **Time** ....

Travel BINGO
Highway

Travel BINGO Highway

Travel BINGO Highway

Name .... Time ....

Travel BINGO Highway

Name .... **Time** ....

Travel BINGO Highway

Name .... Time ....

Travel BINGO Highway

Name		Time		

Travel BINGO Highway

Name	....	Time	....

Travel BINGO
Highway

Travel BINGO
Highway

Travel BINGO
Highway

Name .... Time ....

Travel BINGO Highway

Name .... Time ....

Travel BINGO
Highway

| Name | .... | Time | .... |

Name .... **Time** ....

Travel BINGO
🛣 Highway

Travel BINGO
Highway

Name .... **Time** ....

Travel BINGO
🛣 Highway

Name .... **Time** ....

Travel BINGO
Highway

Travel BINGO Highway

Travel BINGO Highway

Travel BINGO
Highway

Travel BINGO Highway

Travel BINGO Highway

Travel BINGO
Highway

Travel BINGO Highway

Name .... Time ....

Travel BINGO Highway

Travel BINGO
Highway

Name .... **Time** ....

Travel BINGO Highway

Name .... Time ....

Travel BINGO Highway

Name .... **Time** ....

Travel BINGO
Highway

Name .... Time ....

Travel BINGO Highway

Name	Time

Travel BINGO

Highway

Travel BINGO Highway

Name .... **Time** ....

Travel BINGO
Highway

Name .... Time ....

Travel BINGO
Highway

Name .... Time ....

Travel BINGO Highway

Name .... Time ....

Name .... **Time** ....

  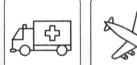

Travel BINGO
Highway

Travel BINGO Highway

Travel BINGO
Highway

Name .... Time ....

Travel BINGO Highway

Name .... **Time** ....

Travel BINGO Highway

Name .... **Time** ....

Travel BINGO Highway

Name .... **Time** ....

Travel BINGO Highway

Travel BINGO

🛣 Highway

Name .... **Time** ....

Travel BINGO
Highway

Travel BINGO Highway

Travel BINGO
Highway

Travel BINGO
Highway

Travel BINGO Highway

Travel BINGO
Highway

Name .... Time ....

Travel BINGO Highway

Travel BINGO Highway

Name .... Time ....

Travel BINGO Highway

Travel BINGO Highway

Name .... **Time** ....

Travel BINGO Highway

Travel BINGO

Highway

Name .... Time ....

Travel BINGO
Highway

Travel BINGO

Highway

Name .... Time ....

Travel BINGO Highway

Travel BINGO
Highway

Name .... Time ....

Travel BINGO
Highway

Name .... Time ....

Travel BINGO Highway

Name .... **Time** ....

Travel BINGO
Highway

Name .... Time ....

Travel BINGO Highway

Name			Time	

Travel BINGO
Highway

Travel BINGO
Highway

Name .... Time ....

Travel BINGO Highway

Travel BINGO
Highway

Name .... Time ....

Travel BINGO Highway

Name .... **Time** ....

Travel BINGO
Highway

Name .... Time ....

Travel BINGO Highway

Travel BINGO Highway

Name .... **Time** ....

Travel BINGO Highway

Name .... **Time** ....

Travel BINGO Highway

Travel BINGO
Highway

Name .... Time ....

Travel BINGO Highway

Name .... Time ....

Travel BINGO
Highway

Travel BINGO Highway

Travel BINGO Highway

Travel BINGO
Highway

Travel BINGO
Highway

Name .... Time ....

Travel BINGO
Highway

Name .... **Time** ....

Travel BINGO Highway

Travel BINGO
Highway

Made in the USA
Monee, IL
22 July 2025

21655168R00075